Essence of Turkey

Uncovering Unique Itineraries

Nomad Notes

All contents, including text, images, and illustrations, in the travel guidebooks published under the brand "Nomad Notes" are protected by copyright laws. The author and publisher have taken every effort to ensure the accuracy and reliability of the information provided in these guidebooks. However, they cannot be held responsible for any errors, omissions, or consequences arising from the use of this material.

No part of these guidebooks may be reproduced, distributed, or transmitted in any form or by any means, including photocopying, recording, or other electronic or mechanical methods, without the prior written permission of the publisher, except in the case of brief quotations embodied in critical reviews and certain other noncommercial uses permitted by copyright law.

Readers are advised to use the information provided in these guidebooks at their own discretion. The author and publisher shall not be liable for any loss, injury, or inconvenience arising from the use or reliance on the information contained in these guidebooks.

The "Nomad Notes" brand name, logo, and associated trademarks are the property of the publisher and may not be used without prior written permission.

For inquiries or permissions requests, please contact the publisher.

Copyright © 2023 by Nomad Notes.

All rights reserved.

Turkey is a country with a rich history, diverse culture, and stunning landscapes. Located at the crossroads of Asia and Europe, it has been home to many ancient civilizations and empires that have left their mark on its culture and history. Modern Turkey was founded in 1923 by Mustafa Kemal Ataturk, who transformed the country from an empire to a republic.

Anatolia, the Asian part of Turkey, was home to many ancient civilizations and empires such as the Hittites, Persians, Greeks, and Romans. The Turks, a Turkic nomadic people from Central Asia migrated to Anatolia in the 11th century and established the Seljuk Empire. The Ottoman Turks ruled over a vast empire for over 600 years; they were also from Central Asia and left a lasting legacy on Turkish culture and history.

Today's Turkish schoolchildren learn about their country's rich history and culture through textbooks that cover topics such as the Ottoman Empire, Turkish Republic, Turkic nomads, among others. However, experiencing Turkey's wonders first-hand is an entirely different experience.

This is where "Turkey Unveiled" comes into play - it is a unique travel guide that unravels all of Turkey's wonders. With its detailed descriptions of various destinations across Turkey accompanied by stunning photographs; this book provides readers with an opportunity to experience Turkey like never before.

The book covers all aspects of travel within Turkey - from historical sites such as Ephesus to natural wonders like Cappadocia's fairy chimneys or Pamukkale's white terraces. It also includes reviews of hotels and restaurants across the country so readers can plan their trip accordingly.

What makes "Turkey Unveiled" stand out is its focus on off-the-beaten-path destinations that are often overlooked by traditional guidebooks. These hidden gems offer travelers an authentic glimpse into Turkish life while avoiding crowds of tourists found in more popular destinations.

"Turkey Unveiled" is not just a travel guide; it's an invitation to explore Turkey's culture, history, and natural beauty. It provides readers with the tools they need to plan their trip while inspiring them to step out of their comfort zone and discover something new.

Table of Contents

TURKEY: A CULTURAL KALEIDOSCOPE 1

A Rich History Dating Back to Ancient Times............ 3

Diverse Cultural Influences 5

Today's Modern And Vibrant Country....................... 6

Practicalities And Essential Information 9

Visa Requirements.. 9

Currency.. 10

Safety.. 10

Transportation Options.............................. 11

Shopping in Turkey................................. 11

Objective Safety Considerations 12

Seasonal Variations and Climate Overview............ 12

Recommended packing list 14

Unconventional Itineraries 16

Whirlwind Adventure............................... 18

Istanbul's historic landmarks, Cappadocia's surreal landscapes, and Ephesus' ancient ruins...................... 19

Paragliding or hot air ballooning 20

Optimizing time and transportation logistics............ 21

Whirlwind Trip 22

Beyond the Itinerary 29

Whirling Dervishes Ceremony in Konya 31

Best Places to Visit in Turkey 33

Blue Mosque 34

Cotton Castle hot springs 34

The Fairy Chimneys of Cappadocia 35

The pools of Pamukkale 36

Blue Lagoon, Olüdeniz 36

Gümüşlük, Bodrum 37

The domes of Istanbul 38

Patara 39

Kaş 39

Ephesus 40

Butterfly Valley, Fethiye 41

Dalyan 41

Anadolu Kavağı 42

Istanbul 42

Cappadocia 43

Pamukkale 43

Balat, Istanbul *44*

Selimiye Mosque, Edirne *45*

Troy *45*

Kas *46*

Topkapi Palace *46*

Closing Thoughts 47

APPENDICES 48

Useful phrases in Turkish and a basic language guide48

Directory of recommended accommodations, restaurants, and tour operators *49*

Hotels in Turkey For Travelers *49*

List of Recommended 20 Restaurants in Turkey *52*

List of Recommended 20 Tour Operators In Turkey. *54*

NOMAD NOTES 57

TURKEY: A CULTURAL KALEIDOSCOPE

Turkey is a country of cultural richness and diversity, boasting an incredible mix of ancient civilizations, stunning landscapes, and vibrant urban centers. From the bustling streets of Istanbul to the awe-inspiring Cappadocia, Turkey is a destination that offers something for everyone.

Hagia Sophia is one of the most iconic ancient sites in Turkey, and a must see for any history buff visiting the country. This 6th-century Byzantine church-turned-mosque has been standing since 537 AD, and is renowned for its architecture and religious significance.

Ottoman conquest in 1453. Once inside, visitors can admire its stunning mosaics and impressive dome, which is said to be the largest in the world.

Turkey is also home to some of the world's most spectacular outdoor scenery. From the stunning Mediterranean coastline to the majestic mountains of Cappadocia, Turkey offers an amazing variety of natural beauty for travelers to explore and enjoy. Take a dip in one of Turkey's many crystal-clear turquoise waters or take a hike up one of the country's many mountains for unparalleled views.

Those looking for an urban adventure will find plenty to do in Turkey's many vibrant cities and towns. Istanbul is perhaps the most famous destination, offering unparalleled shopping opportunities, mouthwatering cuisine, and a unique blend of European and Middle Eastern cultures. Other cities like Ankara, Izmir, and Antalya are also worth exploring for their own unique attractions.

Turkey Unveiled

From ancient ruins to modern metropolises, Turkey has something to offer everyone. Whether you're looking for relaxation or adventure, this cultural kaleidoscope will provide plenty of unforgettable memories!

A Rich History Dating Back to Ancient Times

Today, visitors of Turkey can explore its many ancient sites and monuments. From the well-preserved ruins of Ephesus to the majestic Hagia Sophia, travelers can experience firsthand the beauty and grandeur of Turkey's past. There are also several important archaeological sites such as Gobekli Tepe, which date back over 12,000 years and provide an incredible insight into life during antiquity.

Turkey Unveiled

For those interested in more recent history, Turkey is also home to countless museums and galleries that showcase some of the country's most impressive artworks. Istanbul's Topkapi Palace Museum is a must-see for any history-lover visiting the city, while Ankara's Anatolian Civilizations Museum offers a fascinating glimpse into Turkey's various cultural influences throughout its long history.

Turkey is blessed with an abundance of natural beauty that will leave you feeling inspired and awestruck. The country has a mix of both captivating coastlines and majestic mountains, making it perfect for outdoor adventurers looking for a unique variety of landscapes to explore.

The Mediterranean coastline provides plenty of opportunities for sunbathing or swimming in crystal clear waters while trekking through lush forests or climbing one of its many mountains offer unparalleled views. Cappadocia is especially famous for its unique rock formations and hot air balloons rides offering stunning aerial views day or night.

Turkey Unveiled

Whether you're looking for relaxation on sandy beaches or excitement in rugged mountain trails, there's something here to suit everyone's tastes!

Diverse Cultural Influences

Turkey is a country that has been influenced by many different cultures throughout its history. From the ancient Greeks to the modern Turks, the culture and traditions of Turkey have been shaped by many different civilizations over time.

The influence of the Greeks can be seen in many aspects of Turkish life, including architecture and cuisine. Greek influences can also be seen in some forms of music, dance, theater, and literature. Greek Orthodox Christianity is also still practiced in some parts of the country.

The influence of the Ottomans can be seen in many aspects of Turkish life as well, particularly in terms of art, architecture, language, and cuisine. The Ottoman Empire played an important role in shaping modern Turkey and its identity, which is why it is still so evident today.

Turkey Unveiled

Today's Modern And Vibrant Country

Turkish cuisine

Turkish cuisine is one of the world's oldest and most diverse culinary cultures. With influences from the Middle East, Central Asia, Greece, and the Balkans, Turkish food offers a wide variety of flavors and dishes to explore. From popular kebabs to traditional desserts, Turkish cuisine is sure to satisfy any traveler's palate.

Popular dishes include meze platters, which are a selection of small dishes served as an appetizer, and pide bread, which is similar to pizza. Another must-try dish is lahmacun, a thin flatbread topped with minced meat and herbs.

Turkish art

Turkish art has been influenced by the country's rich cultural heritage. From ancient mosaics found in archaeological sites to modern contemporary art galleries in major cities , there is something here to suit every art enthusiast.

Traditional Turkish music and dance

Turkey has a long and vibrant history of traditional music and dance that continue to be practiced today. Popular forms of traditional music include the baglama (string instrument) and saz (plucked instrument). Traditional dances such as horon, halay, and zeybek are popular at weddings and other celebrations.

Rich Cultural Customs

Turkey is a country full of cultural customs that are sure to fascinate and intrigue any traveler. One such custom is the tradition of hospitality, which is deeply embedded in

Turkey Unveiled

Turkish culture. It's not uncommon for people to offer visitors food and drink, which is meant as a gesture of welcome and respect. Another traditional custom is the usage of salt and bread on the table, which symbolizes the importance of sharing in Turkish culture.

Travelers to Turkey will be sure to experience a culture full of hospitality and rich traditions that will stay with them long after their visit.

Traditional customs

Turkish culture is full of unique traditions and customs. For example, it is traditional for a bride to wear a red wedding dress, which symbolizes fertility and happiness. Turkish hospitality is also renowned throughout the world, with visitors being welcomed into homes and treated as one of the family.

PRACTICALITIES AND ESSENTIAL INFORMATION

For visitors to Turkey, there are a few practicalities and essential information that they should be aware of.

Visa Requirements

If you plan on traveling to Turkey, it is important to know the visa requirements needed for entry. Depending on which country you are coming from, the visa requirements may vary. Most travelers will need a passport and a valid travel visa or e-visa in order to enter Turkey.

Citizens of most European countries can enter Turkey without a visa if they intend to stay in the country for less than 90 days.

Currency

The official currency of Turkey is the Turkish lira (TRY). Major credit cards and debit cards are widely accepted throughout the country, although it is always best to carry some local currency as well. ATMs are widely available in most cities and towns.

Safety

Turkey is generally a safe destination for travelers, but it is important to be aware of your surroundings and not put yourself in any dangerous situations. Be sure to take normal safety precautions, such as avoiding walking alone at night and keeping your valuables secure.

Transportation Options

When it comes to transportation within Turkey, visitors have numerous options. The most common form of transport is by road, with buses, taxis and car rentals being the most popular. Buses are the favored mode of transport for many travelers as they are cheap and convenient. Taxis are a great option for those who want more flexibility and privacy but can be quite expensive depending on where you're traveling.

Shopping in Turkey

Travelers to Turkey will find plenty of places to shop and explore. From the bustling bazaars of Istanbul to the charming boutiques of Ankara, there are many places to hunt for souvenirs, traditional handicrafts, and unique finds. Popular items include carpets, jewelry, pottery, spices, Turkish delight (lokum), and kilim rugs.

Objective Safety Considerations

When traveling to Turkey, there are some important safety considerations to keep in mind. The country has experienced political and security issues in recent years, and visitors should stay aware of their surroundings. It is recommended that travelers check the U.S. State Department's website for any travel advisories before planning their trip, as well as current news reports on the region.

In general, it is best to avoid demonstrations and large public gatherings. Additionally, visitors should keep important documents such as passports and visas in a secure location, as they are targets for theft.

Seasonal Variations and Climate Overview

Turkey is known for its diverse climate and seasonal variations. With four distinct seasons, each season provides unique experiences for travelers.

Turkey Unveiled

Spring is an ideal time to visit Turkey as the weather is mild and generally sunny. The temperatures begin to rise in March, with April and May being the warmest months of the spring season with temperatures ranging from 18 degrees Celsius (64 F) to 24 degrees Celsius (75 F).

Summer is the warmest season in Turkey and temperatures can reach up to 40 degrees Celsius (104 F) in some areas. It is best to avoid traveling during the summer months if you are not used to high temperatures.

Fall brings cooler weather, with temperatures ranging from 12 degrees Celsius (54F) to 20 degrees Celsius (68F). The autumn colors of the trees make this season a beautiful time to visit.

Winter is the coldest season in Turkey, but temperatures are relatively mild compared to other countries in Europe. Average temperatures range from 2 degrees Celsius (36 F) to 12 degrees Celsius (54F). Snowfall is possible in some areas of the country, so it is best to check local weather forecasts before traveling during the winter months.

Recommended packing list

When preparing to travel to Turkey, it's important to ensure you have all the necessary items for a successful trip. Here is a recommended packing list for your trip to Turkey:

Clothing: Make sure to bring light, breathable clothing that you can layer when necessary. Pack long pants and tops that cover your arms and legs as Turkish culture is conservative. Also be sure to bring a light sweater for cooler evenings.

Shoes: Comfortable walking shoes are essential for exploring Turkey's many sights.

Head wear: Bring a hat or scarf to protect your head from the sun and dust.

Toiletries: Don't forget items such as sunscreen, insect repellent, and lip balm.

Power adapter: Bring a power adapter if you're bringing any electronics with you.

Travel documents: Bring your passport, visa (if required), and any other necessary travel documents.

Turkey Unveiled

Money: Make sure to have some cash on hand in case credit cards and ATM machines are not available.

Cultural Tips: When traveling to Turkey, it's important to respect the local culture and customs. A few key points to remember include:

Greeting: When greeting someone, use both hands when shaking hands and maintain eye contact.

Dress code: Dress modestly in public spaces, avoiding clothing that is too revealing or tight-fitting.

Cultural Customs and Etiquette: When visiting religious sites, ensure that you are dressed appropriately and keep your voice down. Shoes must be removed when entering mosques. Additionally, it is important to be mindful of the local customs and not take pictures without permission, especially in rural areas.

When traveling to Turkey, it is important to be aware of the cultural etiquette in order to ensure a pleasant trip. Generally speaking, Turks are friendly and welcoming people, but there are still certain customs and courtesies that it is best to adhere to.

If invited into someone's home, it is polite to take off your shoes upon entering, even if not asked. When greeting someone, a handshake is appropriate with men, and a hug or kiss on the cheek with women. Avoid physical contact with members of the opposite sex that you do not know. Additionally, it is considered rude to point at someone or something; use an open hand instead.

Be sure to research further cultural customs before your trip in order to make sure you have a great experience in Turkey!

UNCONVENTIONAL ITINERARIES

The travelers who are looking for something different, however, unconventional itineraries based on the duration of the trip can be a great way to experience the best this country has to offer.

For those who are visiting Turkey for a shorter period of time, an unconventional itinerary can be a great way to make the most of their trip. A short trip may not allow enough time to explore all of the historic sites in Istanbul or Ephesus, but there is still plenty to see and do. One option is to take a cruise along the Mediterranean coast, stopping at several different ports and exploring some of the stunning beaches and quaint towns along the way. Another great option for short trips is to explore the country's diverse landscape by taking a road trip through Turkey's countryside. This allows travelers to get away from the hustle and bustle of cities like Istanbul and experience rural life in the beautiful mountain and coastal towns of Turkey.

For those who are lucky enough to be able to stay in Turkey for an extended period, there are plenty of unconventional itineraries to keep them busy. One option is to spend some time exploring the country's many ancient cities, such as Ephesus, Hierapolis , and Troy. Another great option is to take a hot air balloon ride over Cappadocia's stunning landscape, or explore the caves and underground cities in the region. For those who are looking for something a bit more adventurous, white water rafting on the Coruh River is another great way to experience Turkey's natural beauty. Finally, no trip to Turkey would be complete without a visit to one of the country's many thermal springs, such as Pamukkale or Afyonkarahisar.

Whirlwind Adventure

Turkey Unveiled

If you're looking for a fast-paced, adrenaline-fueled adventure, Turkey should be on the top of your list. You can get your heart racing with white water rafting on the Coruh River or take an ATV tour of Cappad ocia's lunar landscape. You can also go paragliding in Pamukkale or take a hot air balloon ride over the stunning valleys and rock formations of the region. Don't forget to stop by some of Turkey's historical sites such as the ruins at Ephesus or the terraced pools at Hierapolis.

Istanbul's historic landmarks, Cappadocia's surreal landscapes, and Ephesus' ancient ruins.

Start your journey in Istanbul, exploring the city's traditional bazaars and grand mosques. Then head to Ephesus to explore some of the world's best preserved ancient ruins, and afterwards take a hot air balloon ride over Cappadocia's surreal rock formations.

If you're looking for a more relaxed, reflective experience while exploring Turkey, there are plenty of options. Spend some time relaxing at one of Turkey's many thermal springs such as Afyonkarahisar or Pamukkale, both of which provide a perfect opportunity to soak in the country's stunning scenery. You can also explore some of Turkey's rural villages and experience life away from the hustle and bustle of cities like Istanbul.

Paragliding or hot air ballooning

Paragliding is one of the most popular activities in the country, and it gives visitors a chance to soar above some of Turkey's stunning landscapes. Some of the best places for paragliding include Oludeniz, Kusadasi, and Antalya. Each destination has its own unique sites to explore.

Hot air balloon rides are also available in some areas, giving visitors a chance to float above Cappadocia's surreal rock formations and stunning valleys. If you're looking for an even more thrilling experience, white water rafting on the Coruh River is a great way to get your heart pumping.

Optimizing time and transportation logistics

For those looking to experience as much as possible in a short amount of time, we recommend focusing on optimizing time and transportation logistics. This includes booking overnight flights or high-speed trains to cut down on travel time, using local transportation such as ferries or buses to get around quickly and cheaply, and taking advantage of discounts on attractions and transportation.

To make the most of your time, prioritize the most popular attractions such as Istanbul's historic landmarks, Cappadocia's surreal landscapes, and Ephesus' ancient ruins. If you have more time, explore some of the region's smaller villages or take a guided tour to get off the beaten path.

Whirlwind Trip

If you only have a few days to explore Turkey, there are some must-see attractions that you should prioritize during your visit.

Start off in Istanbul, where you can get a real taste of the country's history and culture. Check out the iconic Hagia Sophia, the former Greek Orthodox church turned mosque that is now an architectural wonder and home to some of Turkey's most stunning mosaics. From there, head to the Blue Mosque, with its striking blue-tiled exterior and six minarets. Don't forget to stop by the Grand Bazaar or take a boat across the Bosphorus Strait for unique views of Istanbul's skyline.

For a more reflective experience, plan a trip to Cappadocia and Ephesus. In Cappadocia, take a hot air ba``1lloon ride over the surreal rock formations or visit one of the region's underground cities. And in Ephesus, explore some of the world's best preserved ancient ruins.

Cultural Immersion: Deeper Exploration of Local Markets and Hidden Gems

There are so many things to see and do in this vibrant metropolis—from its iconic landmarks to its hidden neighborhoods, local markets, and secret gems.

Exploring Istanbul's neighborhoods will give you a better understanding of its culture and history. Take a stroll through the winding alleyways of Sultanahmet, the heart of Old City Istanbul, or wander through the lively streets of **Karaköy and Beyoğlu.** Here you will find an array of interesting shops, cafes, and restaurants, all offering unique insights into Turkish culture and cuisine.

For a deeper cultural experience, explore some of Istanbul's many markets. The Grand Bazaar is the city's largest and most famous market, with over 5,000 shops selling everything from jewelry to spices. For something more off the beaten path, visit some of Istanbul's smaller markets such as the Spice Bazaar or Balat Market for a unique shopping experience.

Finally, take some time to explore some of **Istanbul's hidden gems**. From underground baths to secret gardens, there are plenty of unique places to discover in this city. Don't forget to visit some of the city's rooftop bars for stunning views of Istanbul's skyline and a unique perspective on the city.

Turkey is a country with a rich and diverse culture, offering travelers unique experiences in every aspect of their visit. From the traditional music to the culinary delights, there are plenty of ways to immerse yourself in Turkish culture. Here are some recommendations for experiencing some of Turkey's most treasured customs.

The Turkish baths, or hamams, have long been revered as a place of relaxation and socialization. Take a visit to one of Istanbul's historic hamams for a unique cultural experience.

To get an authentic taste of Turkish music, look no further than Istanbul's many traditional cafés, or meyhanes. Here

Turkey Unveiled

you can listen to live performances of traditional Anatolian folk music while enjoying some traditional food and drinks. And for culinary delights , sample some of Turkey's most beloved dishes such as kebab, borek, and baklava.

For those looking to explore beyond the popular attractions, there are several remarkable ancient sites scattered throughout the country that offer a unique insight into Turkey's long and rich history.

Troy, located in northwest Turkey near the Aegean Sea, is the legendary site of the Trojan War. The ruins of this ancient city are still standing today, offering visitors the chance to explore its fascinating history.

Turkey Unveiled

Mount Nemrut, located in southeast Turkey near the Syrian border, is also worth a visit. This ancient mountain sanctuary is home to several giant statues dating back over two thousand years and offers spectacular views across the surrounding landscape.

If you're looking for a truly unique experience, then consider booking a stay at one of Turkey's many luxury hotels. From boutique seaside resorts to traditional Ottoman mansions, there is something for everyone in the country's accommodation options. For the ultimate in relaxation, try an all-inclusive spa resort where you can indulge in massages and other treatments.

Turkey Unveiled

For outdoor enthusiasts, there are plenty of opportunities for adventure in Turkey. From trekking through the rugged landscape of Cappadocia to exploring the depths of Saklikent Gorge, there is something to do for every type of traveler.

Off the Beaten Path: Discovering Offbeat Destinations

If you're looking for a unique vacation destination, then look no further than Eastern Anatolia in Turkey. Located in the far east of the country, it is home to some of the most rugged and untouched landscapes that will take your breath away. Enjoy hikes through lush valleys and mountains, explore ancient ruins and archaeological sites, or take a boat ride along the river Tigris.

Eastern Anatolia also offers a glimpse into the culture and heritage of its Kurdish population. From visiting traditional villages in the mountains to exploring bustling towns like Diyarbakir, there are plenty of experiences to be had here. Don't forget to sample some of the region's local cuisine, from mezzes and flatbreads to grilled meats and savory pastries. For an unforgettable adventure, Eastern Anatolia is the perfect offbeat destination.

Turkey Unveiled

Turkey offers a range of outdoor activities that can be experienced in its many diverse landscapes. From hiking routes through **lush forests,** to visits to remote **monasteries** and encounters with nomadic communities, Turkey has something for everyone.

For hikers, Turkey offers some of the finest walking trails in Europe. The Lycian Way is one of the most popular routes, taking walkers through some of Turkey's most spectacular landscapes. There are also several routes that take you across the majestic Taurus Mountains and into the remote valleys of Cappadocia.

The Black Sea coast of Turkey is one of the country's lesser explored regions, offering visitors a chance to explore an area steeped in centuries of history and culture. The region is bordered by Bulgaria to the east and Georgia to the north, while stunning mountain landscapes dominate much of its interior.

One of the most popular destinations on the Black Sea coast is the ancient city of **Zeugma,** a UNESCO World Heritage Site that was founded in the 3rd century BC. Visitors can explore vast ruins of villas and temples, as well as view the world-famous mosaics which are still intact today.

BEYOND THE ITINERARY

Turkey has a lot to offer beyond the usual tourist itinerary. From ancient cities and monuments to awe-inspiring landscapes, Turkey is an exciting place to explore.

For nature lovers, Turkey offers breathtaking scenery. From the snowcapped mountains of Anatolia to the forests of the Black Sea region, there are plenty of opportunities for outdoor adventure in this diverse country. Hiking and trekking through the countryside is a great way to explore the region and discover its hidden gems.

Turkey is also home to many cultural attractions. The country has a rich history, with monuments and ruins that tell the story of centuries past. Tourists can visit ancient cities like Ephesus and Troy, or explore some of Turkey's incredible archaeological sites like Göbekli Tepe.

Turkey Unveiled

Visit the Ancient City of Ephesus

Ephesus, an ancient city located in present day Turkey, is a must-see for any traveler looking to explore the rich history and culture of this beautiful country. The ruins of Ephesus are among some of the best preserved in the world and offer visitors a glimpse into the grandeur of classical antiquity.

The ancient city was once one of the largest Mediterranean cities in antiquity and home to the Temple of Artemis, one of the Seven Wonders of the World. Today, visitors can explore the remains of its grand amphitheater, temples and other ruins while learning about its fascinating history.

Take a Hot Air Balloon Ride over Cappadocia. Cappadocia is one of Turkey's most spectacular destinations. The region is renowned for its unique lunar landscape, comprised of towering rock formations and surreal underground cities. One of the best ways to experience Cappadocia's beauty is to take a hot air balloon ride, which will give you an unforgettable view of the region .

Turkey Unveiled

Explore Istanbul's Bazaars and Markets

Istanbul has some of the most vibrant and exciting bazaars and markets in the world. From bustling street markets to grand covered bazaars, these places offer an invaluable insight into Turkish culture and society.

The Grand Bazaar is the largest and oldest bazaar in Istanbul, first established in 1461. It's a warren of over 4000 shops spread across 61 streets, selling everything from traditional Turkish carpets to jewelry and spices. Another popular destination is the Spice Bazaar, where you can pick up all kinds of delicious ingredients for your cooking.

Whirling Dervishes Ceremony in Konya

Turkey Unveiled

Konya is home to one of the most famous ceremonies in Turkey – The Whirling Dervishes Ceremony. This mesmerizing show has been taking place for centuries and is a must-see for any visitor to the city. During the ceremony, Sufi musicians provide stirring music while the dervishes perform their traditional whirling dance in perfect unison. The ceremony is a beautiful and moving experience, and one that will stay with you for a long time.

Aside from the wonderful attractions that can be found within Turkey, there are also plenty of exciting side trips and day excursions to neighboring countries or islands.

For those looking for a bit of adventure, a visit to the Greek island of Rhodes is a must. This idyllic island offers an abundance of activities and sightseeing opportunities, from exploring the ancient ruins of Rhodes to lounging on its beautiful beaches.

For a cultural experience unlike any other, hop over to Istanbul for a few days. This vibrant city is home to stunning architecture, bustling markets, and plenty of museums and galleries to explore. Make sure to include stops at iconic landmarks such as the Blue Mosque and Topkapi Palace .

For a truly unique destination, head to the Greek island of Chios. This charming isle is known for its mastic villages and pine forests, as well as its rich history and culture. Enjoy the local cuisine, wander through winding alleys, or simply relax on the beach – whatever you choose to do, Chios promises an unforgettable experience.

BEST PLACES TO VISIT IN TURKEY

Turkey is an incredible destination for travelers looking to experience a unique combination of Eastern and Western culture, ancient history, and stunning natural beauty. From the country's bustling cities to its ancient ruins, there are plenty of exciting places to explore in Turkey. Here are some of the best places to visit in Turkey:

Blue Mosque

The Blue Mosque in Istanbul is an iconic symbol of Turkey's rich history and culture. Located in the heart of the city, it was built by Sultan Ahmet I between 1609 and 1616 and is one of the most impressive examples of Ottoman architecture. Inside, thousands of tiny blue tiles give the mosque its name, while its courtyard houses a fountain for ritual ablutions and four min arets.

No visit to Istanbul is complete without a visit to the Blue Mosque – it's one of the most iconic sights in the city and an absolute must-see.

Cotton Castle hot springs

The stunning Cotton Castle hot springs, located in the Denizli province of southwestern Turkey, are a must-see for any traveler to the region. Tucked amidst the majestic Taurus Mountains, this natural wonder is a sight to behold and provides its visitors with a once-in-a-lifetime experience.

Cotton Castle hot springs are fed by 17 separate geothermal sources that emerge from the mountainside. The warm, mineral-rich waters pool into terraced basins that cascade down the hillside, giving them their otherworldly appearance.

Visiting Cotton Castle is a truly magical experience – bathe in the warm waters and take in the stunning views of the surrounding landscape as you relax and unwind.

The Fairy Chimneys of Cappadocia

The Fairy Chimneys of Cappadocia in Turkey are one of the country's most iconic natural wonders. Located in the central Anatolian region, this area is known for its bizarre rock formations that have been carved out by thousands of years of wind and water erosion. The result is an awe-inspiring landscape dotted with hundreds of cone-shaped towers, or fairy chim neys, that are a sight to behold.

Exploring the Fairy Chimneys of Cappadocia is a truly unique experience – take in the views as you wander through this remarkable landscape and learn about its rich history.

The pools of Pamukkale

Pamukkale, meaning "cotton castle" in Turkish, is one of the most popular travel destinations in Turkey. Located in the Denizli Province of southwestern Anatolia, Pamukkale's white terraces and thermal pools are a stunning sight to behold.

The terraces of Pamukkale were created by hot springs that rise from the ground at a temperature of 35C (95F). The hot waters deposit calcium-rich travertine onto the terraces, which gives them their stunning white color.

Visiting Pamukkale is an unforgettable experience – take a dip in its thermal pools and marvel at its stunning landscape.

Blue Lagoon, Olüdeniz

The Blue Lagoon in Olüdeniz is one of the most popular tourist attractions in Turkey. Located on the south-western coast of the Turkish Mediterranean, near Fethiye, this stunning lagoon is renowned for its crystal clear turquoise waters and beautiful white sandy beaches. The Blue Lagoon is a protected area due to its unique ecology, with a wide variety of flora and fauna making it a nature lover's paradise.

Sailing, snorkeling, and swimming are all popular activities at the Blue Lagoon. For those looking for a more relaxed experience, simply take in the stunning views and enjoy some time out in the sun.

Gümüşlük, Bodrum

Gümüşlük, located just outside of Bodrum in the Muğla Province of Turkey, is a stunning coastal town that promises a relaxing and enjoyable holiday for all kinds of travellers. Gümüşlük has become increasingly popular amongst those looking to get away from the hustle and bustle of city life, as it offers an idyllic atmosphere and a laid-back pace of life.

Gümüşlük has something for everyone - take in the stunning views as you wander along the waterfront, enjoy some delicious seafood at one of the many restaurants, or simply spend some time relaxing on the beach. Whatever you do, Gümüşlük is sure to provide an unforgettable holiday experience.

The domes of Istanbul

Istanbul is home to some of the most iconic and beautiful domes in the world. From towering basilicas to opulent mosques, Istanbul's skyline is dotted with these impressive structures.

The city features a variety of incredible domes, ranging from the classic Ottoman-style dome of Hagia Sophia to the majestic dome of Sultanahmet Mosque. These structures are iconic symbols of Istanbul and a must-see for all visitors to the city.

Whether you're exploring on foot or taking in the panoramic views from a boat tour, taking the time to appreciate Istanbul's domes is sure to be an unforgettable experience.

Patara

Patara is a beach town located in the Turkish province of Antalya. It is known for its long, sandy beaches, ancient ruins, and one of the few remaining breeding grounds for loggerhead turtles. Patara is also home to some of the most important archaeological sites in Turkey, including the remains of a Lycian city and an ancient theatre.

The main attraction in Pat ara is its beautiful beach, which stretches for over 10 kilometres and is one of the longest in Turkey. Visitors can sunbathe, swim in the sea or explore the nearby ruins – whatever you choose to do, Patara is sure to provide an unforgettable experience.

Kaş

Kas is a picturesque fishing town located on the Mediterranean coast of Turkey. It's known for its traditional stone buildings, sandy beaches, and stunning sunsets. Kaş is a great destination for visitors looking to experience authentic Turkish culture and the natural beauty of this country.

The city dates back thousands of years and has a diverse history; it was once part of the ancient Ly cian civilization and is now one of the top tourist destinations in Turkey.

Kaş offers a variety of activities for visitors, such as swimming, scuba diving, kayaking, fishing, and boat tours. There are also plenty of restaurants, bars, and shops to explore. Whatever you decide to do in Kas, it's sure to be an unforgettable experience.

Ephesus

Ephesus is one of the most famous historical cities in Turkey. Located on the western coast of the country, it was once the capital of the ancient Roman province of Asia Minor and is now a popular tourist destination for its rich history and spectacular ruins. Ephesus was first settled around 1000 BC and by the 6th century BC, it had become an important trading center along the Aege an coast.

Today, visitors to Ephesus can explore the ruins of temples, theatres, baths, and other structures that date back to ancient times. There's also a selection of museums and galleries that offer insight into the history of this fascinating city. No matter what you choose to do in Ephesus, it's sure to be an unforgettable experience.

Butterfly Valley, Fethiye

Butterfly Valley, located near Fethiye in southwestern Turkey, is a stunning natural wonderland of turquoise colored water, lush green foliage and unique wildlife. The valley is home to the largest butterfly population in Europe; you can view more than 40 species of butterflies here.

The best way to experience Butterfly Valley is to take a boat tour from nearby Fethiye . Here, you'll get to admire the beautiful scenery, watch for wildlife, and explore the hidden coves of the valley. It's a truly unique experience and one that is sure to create lasting memories.

Dalyan

Located in the Mugla province of southwestern Turkey, Dalyan is a stunningly beautiful destination that offers a variety of activities for visitors. As well as being home to some incredible scenery and wildlife, Dalyan is also known for its archaeological sites and hot springs.

One of the most popular attractions in Dalyan is the ancient city of Kaunos, which was once a thriving port. Here, visitors can explore ruins that date back to the 8th century BC and admire the stunning views across the Dalyan River.

Anadolu Kavağı

Anadolu Kavagi is a small fishing village located in Turkey's northern Black Sea region. It's known for its stunning scenery, traditional architecture, and unique culture . Visitors to Anadolu Kavagi can explore the picturesque streets, relax on the beach, and visit nearby attractions such as the Hittite ruins. It's a great place to get away from it all and experience the beauty of rural Turkey.

Istanbul

Istanbul is one of the most fascinating cities in the world. Widely considered the gateway between East and West, this incredible city offers something for everyone; it's home to stunning historical sites, vibrant nightlife, and a diverse range of cultures. Whether you're looking to explore ancient ruins or sample delicious Turkish cuisine, Istanbul has something for you.

Cappadocia

Cappadocia is a stunning region in central Turkey that is renowned for its surreal landscape of rock formations and underground cities. Here, visitors can admire the unique landscapes, explore the ancient cave dwellings, and marvel at the breathtaking views from hot air balloon flights. A visit to Cappadocia is sure to leave you with lasting memories of this captivating part of the country.

Pamukkale

The picturesque town of Pamukkale is located in southwestern Turkey and is renowned for its stunning white cliffs and hot springs. These natural wonders, which are made up of calcium-rich water cascading down the hillside, have been a popular destination since Roman times. Visitors can explore the ruins of the ancient city of Hierapolis and bathe in the thermal pools of Pamukkale.

Balat, Istanbul

Balat is a historic neighborhood in Istanbul, Turkey that has been home to many different cultures throughout its long history. Located on the Golden Horn, this picturesque area of the city has long been important to both religious and artisan communities. With an abundance of beautiful architecture and stunning views of the Bosphorus, Balat is one of the most popular tourist destinations in Istanbul.

One of the highlights of a visit to Balat is the beautiful Aya Yorgi Church, which has stunning views across the city. Other attractions include the Jewish Museum and Fener Greek Orthodox Patriarchate. Exploring the atmospheric streets of Balat is an experience that will stay with you for a long time.

Selimiye Mosque, Edirne

Located in the city of Edirne, the Selimiye Mosque is one of the most impressive examples of Ottoman architecture. Built by renowned architect Mimar Sinan in 1575, this grand mosque features four grand minarets, a stunning marble courtyard, and an intricate collection of domes and arches. It's a must-see for anyone visiting Edirne, and a symbol of the city's rich history.

Troy

Located on the western coast of Turkey, Troy is an ancient city that was once the site of a legendary battle between the Greeks and Trojans. This fascinating archaeological site has been carefully excavated by archeologists, uncovering a wealth of artifacts that tell stories about life in this ancient city. Visitors to Troy can explore the remains of its impressive walls, as well as the nearby ruins of the ancient city of Ilion.

Kas

Kas is a charming coastal town located in the Mediterranean region of Turkey. This stunning destination offers visitors the chance to explore its cobbled streets, enjoy its restaurants and cafes, and relax on its sandy beaches. It's also home to some incredible ruins, such as the ancient Greek amphitheater and a Roman temple . With its unique charm, Kas is a great place to explore the beauty of Turkey's Mediterranean coast.

Topkapi Palace

Topkapi Palace is one of the most iconic landmarks in Istanbul, Turkey. Located on the Seraglio Point near the Bosphorus and Golden Horn, it was once home to the Ottoman Sultans for more than 400 years. Today, visitors can explore its grandeur in all its glory and get a glimpse into the life of these powerful rulers.

The palace complex comprises four main courtyards, each with its own unique features. Visitors can admire the grandeur of its pavilions, mosques, gardens, and fountains as they explore this magnificent palace.

Closing Thoughts

Your journey to Turkey is sure to be a memorable one. From the breathtaking landscapes and ancient ruins, to the colorful culture and vibrant cities, there is something for everyone in this incredible country.

Take the time to explore beyond the tourist attractions and delve into the hidden corners of Turkey. Narrow alleyways lead to secret gardens, bustling bazaars are filled with unique local artifacts, and friendly locals will help you discover the true beauty of this amazing destination. So take a chance, get out there and explore – you never know what hidden gems await!

APPENDICES

Useful phrases in Turkish and a basic language guide

If you are planning on visiting Turkey, it's important to know a few useful phrases in Turkish. There are many languages spoken in the country, but Turkish is the official language and is used by most people. Here is a basic guide to learning some of the basics:

Hello: Merhaba

Goodbye: Hoşça kal

Please: Lütfen

Thank you: Teşekkür ederim

Yes: Evet

No: Hayır

Where is…?: … nerede?

How much is it?: Ne kadar?

Do you speak English?: İngilizce konuşabiliyor musun?

Yes: Eve

Directory of recommended accommodations, restaurants, and tour operators.

Hotels in Turkey For Travelers

If you're looking for a great place to stay in Turkey, there are plenty of options to consider. Whether you're looking for high-end luxury hotels or cozy budget accommodations, there is something to suit every traveler's needs.

For those looking for a luxurious experience, the country offers some of the most lavish and elegant 5-star properties in the world.

For those on a budget, there are also plenty of great 3-star and 4-star hotels that offer excellent value for money. For those looking for a truly unique experience, there is also the option of renting a traditional Turkish house or apartment.

Turkey Unveiled

This is a great way to soak up local culture and get an authentic taste of daily life in Turkey.

List of 20 Best Hotels on Budget In Turkey

Turkey is a beautiful country, full of culture and history. Whether you're looking for an adventure or a relaxing getaway, you can find it in this unique destination. But if you're on a budget, finding the right hotel can be tricky. Fortunately, there are plenty of great hotels to choose from in Turkey that won't break the bank. Here is a list of 20 of the best budget hotels in Turkey:

1. Grand Hotel Ankara

2. Antikhan Istanbul

3. Heaven Hotel, Fethiye

4. Hotel Güneş, Bodrum

5. Alkan Otel, Cappadocia

6. Anjeliq Otel, Istanbul

7. Ozgurluk Pension, K ayseri

Turkey Unveiled

8. Avicenna Hotel, Ankara

9. Ozmen Otel, Izmir

10. Grand Anka Hotel, Istanbul

11. Sehir Palas Hotel, Diyarbakir

12. Sultan Han Hotel, Konya

13. Ekinci Apartments, Istanbul

14. Kent Pension Ankara 15. Grand Kilic Hotel, Ankara

16. Kervansaray Hotel, Konya

17. Aslan Otel, Izmir

18. Alaaddin Hotel, Kayseri

19. Murat Pasha Hotel, Istanbul

20. Erciyes Pension, Kayseri

Turkey Unveiled

List of Recommended 20 Restaurants in Turkey

Turkey is one of the most popular countries for tourists to visit, with its beautiful scenery and rich culture. There are countless places to explore and

experience in Turkey, but one of the best ways to get a taste of the country's flavors and cuisine is by dining at some of its many restaurants. To help you plan your trip, here's a list of 20 recommended restaurants in Turkey:

1. Lokum Istanbul, Istanbul

2. Meze By Lemon Tree, Istanbul

3. Karadeniz, Izmir

4. Asitane Restaurant, Istanbul

5. Zeytinburnu Balikcilik Restaurant, Istanbul

6. Sason Balik Lokantasi, Bodrum

7. Deniz Palas , Istanbul

8. Asmali Cavit, Istanbul

9. Ali Muhiddin Haci Bekir Restaurant, Istanbul

10. Zübeyir Ocakbasi, Istanbul

11. Aspendos, Istanbul

12. Taze Turuncu Balik and Mezesi, Fethiye

13. Keb apci Kadir Usta, Izmir

14. Karadeniz Evi, Ankara

15. Van Kebab and Mezesi, Istanbul

16. Imroz Restaurant, Bodrum

17. Kofteci Ahmet Usta, Istanbul

18. Günaydin Kebapci Restaurant, Ankara

19. Mevlana, Antalya

20. Yanyalı Kebap, Ankara

Turkey Unveiled

List of Recommended 20 Tour Operators In Turkey

Turkey is a wonderful and diverse country with many places to explore and activities to experience. If you're looking for an unforgettable trip in Turkey, it's best to book through a reputable tour operator rather than attempting to do it all yourself. Here's a list of recommended tour operators in Turkey:

1. Travel the Unknown, Istanbul

2. Absolute Travel, Istanbul

3. Let's Go Turkey, Istanbul

4. Go Turkey Tours, Istanbul

5. Destination Middle East, Istanbul

6. Turkish Voyage, Istanbul

7. Imperial Travel Turkey, Istanbul

8. Virikson Holidays, Istanbul

Turkey Unveiled

9. European Tour Services, Istanbul

10. Red Apple Travel Group, Antalya

11. Turista Travel Agency, Ankara

12. My Guide Turkey, Konya

13. Pet radi Travel, Istanbul

14. Turkey Travel Center, Ankara

15. Voyager Tour, Istanbul

16. Cholpan Tours, Istanbul

17. Mediterranean Holidays & Tours, Antalya

18. Gulet Cruise Holidays, Bodrum

19. Turkish Delight Tours, Istanbul

20. Enchanting Travels, Istanbul

Turkey Unveiled

If you're looking to explore some of the amazing attractions that Turkey has to offer, there are plenty of tour operators that can provide you with an unforgettable experience. From discovering historical sites and monuments to experiencing traditional culture, these tour operators will ensure that your trip is a memorable one.

For those looking for adventure, there are several companies offering trekking and rafting trips . They will provide guides and all the necessary equipment, as well as helping you to plan your trips.

For a more relaxing experience, there are companies offering boat tours along Turkey's stunning coastline or hot air balloon rides over Cappadocia. There are also tour operators that can help you immerse yourself in the culture by arranging cooking classes, art classes and visits to popular local markets.

Turkey Unveiled

NOMAD NOTES

Traveling is not just about exploring new places and experiencing different cultures; it's also about embarking on a journey of self-discovery. One of the most rewarding ways to capture these unforgettable moments is through journaling. By putting pen to paper, you can preserve the sights, sounds, and emotions that make each trip unique. Journaling allows you to reflect on your adventures, deepening your connection to the places you visit and the memories you create. So, let the following pages be a canvas for your thoughts, impressions, and personal anecdotes. Feel free to write down your favorite moments, insights, or simply let your pen wander as you relive the joy of your travels. Let these pages become a treasured keepsake, preserving the essence of your journey for years to come. Enjoy this unique space and make it your own. Safe travels!

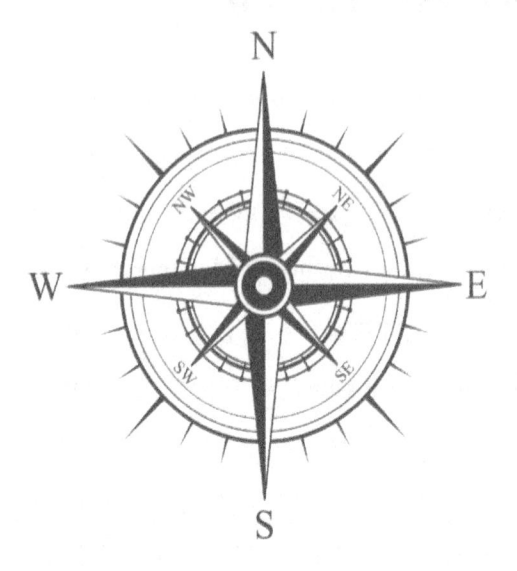

- **It's Time to Travel** -

TRAVEL PLANNER

Date of Trip: ....
Place: ....

TRAVEL BUDGET

Date of Trip: .... Place: ....

Estimated Budget: ....

Description	Category	Cost

Total: ....

	%	SUM
Lodging		
Transportation		
Food:		
Entertainment		
Other		

TRAVEL ITINERARY

Location: ....   Date: ....
                                                   Today Budget: ....

SCHEDULE

07:00   19:00

08:00   20:00

09:00   21:00

10:00   22:00

11:00

12:00
                                                   Breakfast
13:00

14:00

15:00   **Lunch**

16:00

17:00   **Dinner**

18:00

MY DESTINATION

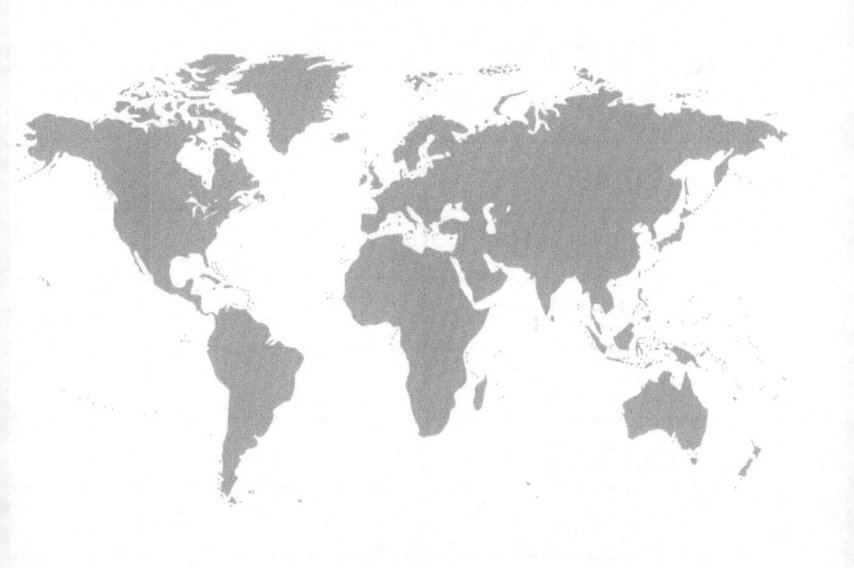

NOTES

ACCOMODATIONS

Hotel	....
Address	....
Contact	....
Booking number	....
Check in	....
Room type	....
Check out	....
Total Nights	....

Rate ☆ ☆ ☆ ☆ ☆

Hotel	....
Address	....
Contact	....
Booking number	....
Check in	....
Room type	....
Check out	....
Total Nights	....

FLIGHT INFORMATION

Flight N° 1

- Airline Name: ....
- Flight N° : ....
- Departure from: ....
- Arrival to: ....
- Duration: ....
- Confirmation: ....

Flight N° 2

- Airline Name: ....
- Flight N° : ....
- Departure from: ....
- Arrival to: ....
- Duration: ....
- Confirmation: ....

Notes

....
....

DON'T FORGET TO PACK

- **Toiletries**
....
....
....
....
....
....
....
....
....
....
....
....
....
....

- **Electronics**
....
....
....
....
....
....
....
....
....
....
....

- **Personal Items**
....
....
....
....
....
....
....
....
....
....
....
....
....
....
....
....
....

- **Medication**
....
....
....
....
....
....
....
....
....
....

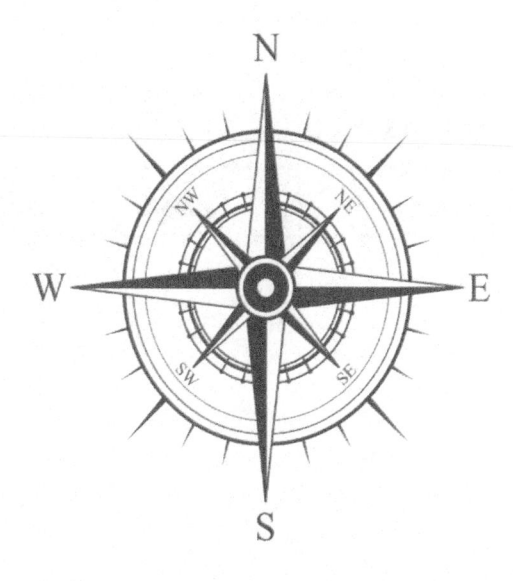

- It's Time to Travel -

TRAVEL PLANNER

Date of Trip: ....
Place: ....

TRAVEL BUDGET

Date of Trip: .... Place: ....

Estimated Budget: ....

Description	Category	Cost

Total:......................

	%	SUM
Lodging		
Transportation		
Food:		
Entertainment		
Other		

TRAVEL ITINERARY

Location: ....   Date: ....
                                                   Today Budget: ....

SCHEDULE

07:00   19:00

08:00   20:00

09:00   21:00

10:00   22:00

11:00

12:00
                                                   Breakfast
13:00

14:00

15:00   **Lunch**

16:00

17:00
                                                   Dinner
18:00

MY DESTINATION

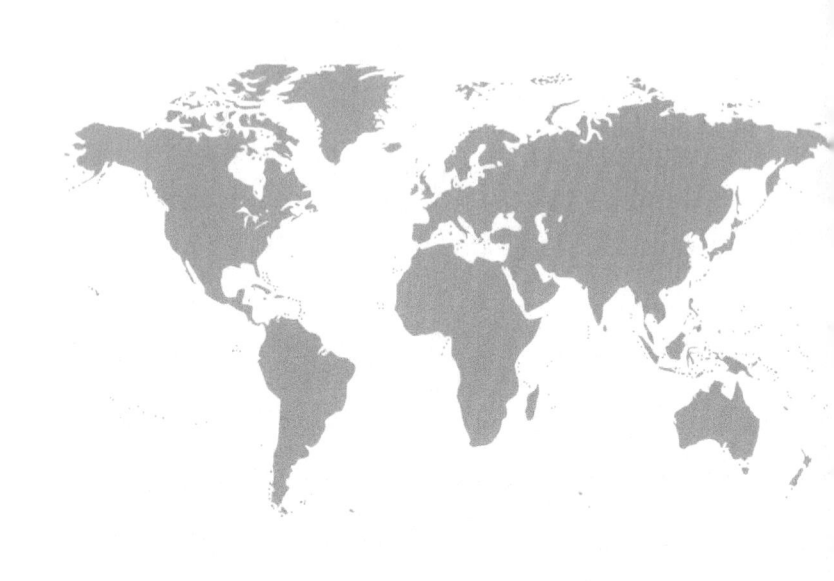

NOTES

ACCOMODATIONS

Hotel	....
Address	....
Contact	....
Booking number	....
Check in	....
Room type	....
Check out	....
Total Nights	....

Rate ☆ ☆ ☆ ☆ ☆

Hotel	....
Address	....
Contact	....
Booking number	....
Check in	....
Room type	....
Check out	....
Total Nights	....

FLIGHT INFORMATION

Flight N° 1

- Airline Name: ....
- Flight N° : ....
- Departure from: ....
- Arrival to: ....
- Duration: ....
- Confirmation: ....

Flight N° 2

- Airline Name: ....
- Flight N° : ....
- Departure from: ....
- Arrival to: ....
- Duration: ....
- Confirmation: ....

Notes

....
....

DON'T FORGET TO PACK

- **Toiletries**

- **Electronics**

- **Personal Items**

- **Medication**

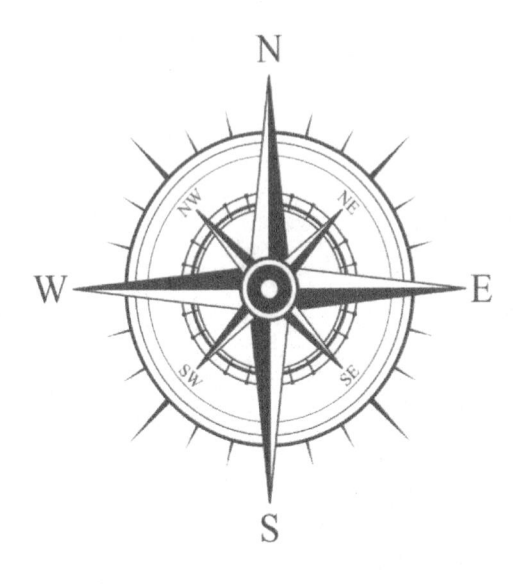

- It's Time to Travel -

TRAVEL PLANNER

Date of Trip: ....
Place: ....

TRAVEL BUDGET

Date of Trip: .... Place: ....

Estimated Budget: ....

Description	Category	Cost

Total: ....

	%	SUM
Lodging		
Transportation		
Food:		
Entertainment		
Other		

TRAVEL ITINERARY

Location: .... Date: ....
Today Budget: ....

SCHEDULE

07:00

08:00

09:00

10:00

11:00

12:00

13:00

14:00

15:00

16:00

17:00

18:00

19:00

20:00

21:00

22:00

Breakfast

Lunch

Dinner

MY DESTINATION

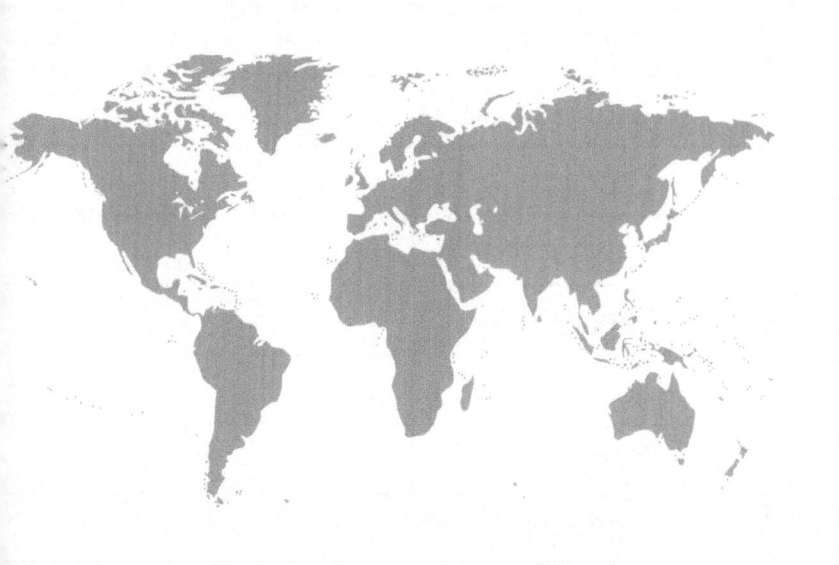

NOTES

ACCOMODATIONS

Hotel	....
Address	....
Contact	....
Booking number	....
Check in	....
Room type	....
Check out	....
Total Nights	....

Rate ☆ ☆ ☆ ☆ ☆

Hotel	....
Address	....
Contact	....
Booking number	....
Check in	....
Room type	....
Check out	....
Total Nights	....

FLIGHT INFORMATION

Flight N° 1

- Airline Name: ....
- Flight N° : ....
- Departure from: ....
- Arrival to: ....
- Duration: ....
- Confirmation: ....

Flight N° 2

- Airline Name: ....
- Flight N° : ....
- Departure from: ....
- Arrival to: ....
- Duration: ....
- Confirmation: ....

Notes
....
....

DON'T FORGET TO PACK

- **Toiletries**

- **Electronics**

- **Personal Items**

- **Medication**

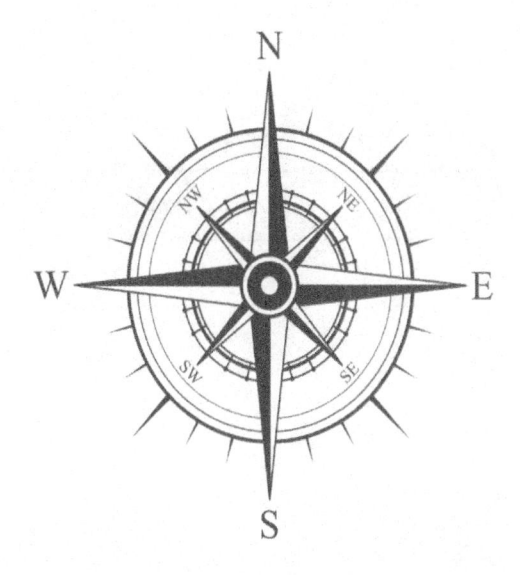

- **It's Time to Travel** -

TRAVEL PLANNER

Date of Trip: ....
Place: ....

TRAVEL BUDGET

Date of Trip: .... Place: ....

Estimated Budget:		
Description	*Category*	*Cost*
	Total:	

	%	SUM
Lodging		
Transportation		
Food:		
Entertainment		
Other		

TRAVEL ITINERARY

Location: ....

Date: ....
Today Budget: ....

SCHEDULE

07:00

08:00

09:00

10:00

11:00

12:00

13:00

14:00

15:00

16:00

17:00

18:00

19:00

20:00

21:00

22:00

Breakfast

Lunch

Dinner

MY DESTINATION

NOTES

ACCOMODATIONS

Hotel	....
Address	....
Contact	....
Booking number	....
Check in	....
Room type	....
Check out	....
Total Nights	....

Rate ☆ ☆ ☆ ☆ ☆

Hotel	....
Address	....
Contact	....
Booking number	....
Check in	....
Room type	....
Check out	....
Total Nights	....

FLIGHT INFORMATION

Flight N° 1

- Airline Name: ....
- Flight N° : ....
- Departure from: ....
- Arrival to: ....
- Duration: ....
- Confirmation: ....

Flight N° 2

- Airline Name: ....
- Flight N° : ....
- Departure from: ....
- Arrival to: ....
- Duration: ....
- Confirmation: ....

Notes
....
....

DON'T FORGET TO PACK

- **Toiletries**

- **Electronics**

- **Personal Items**

- **Medication**

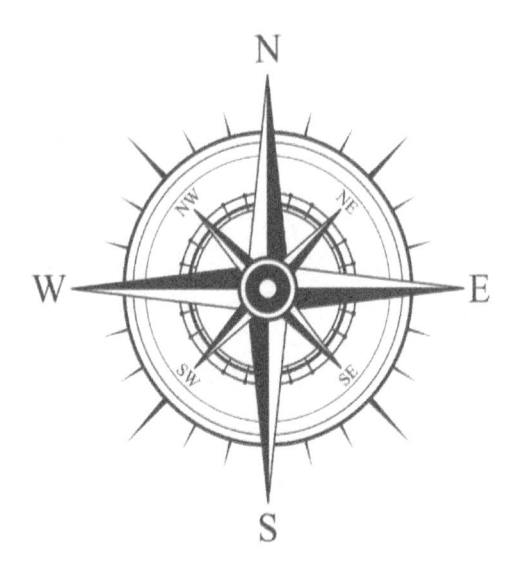

- **It's Time to Travel** -

TRAVEL PLANNER

Date of Trip: ....
Place: ....

TRAVEL BUDGET

Date of Trip: .... Place: ....

Estimated Budget: ....

Description	Category	Cost

Total: ....

	%	SUM
Lodging		
Transportation		
Food:		
Entertainment		
Other		

TRAVEL ITINERARY

Location: ....

Date: ....
Today Budget: ....

SCHEDULE

07:00	19:00
08:00	20:00
09:00	21:00
10:00	22:00
11:00	
12:00	**Breakfast**
13:00	
14:00	
15:00	**Lunch**
16:00	
17:00	**Dinner**
18:00	

MY DESTINATION

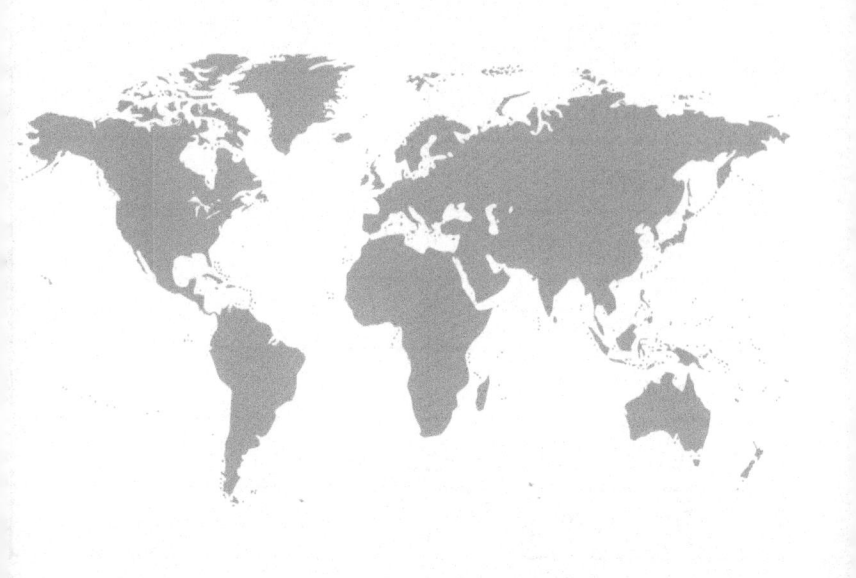

NOTES

ACCOMODATIONS

Hotel	....
Address	....
Contact	....
Booking number	....
Check in	....
Room type	....
Check out	....
Total Nights	....

Rate ☆ ☆ ☆ ☆ ☆

Hotel	....
Address	....
Contact	....
Booking number	....
Check in	....
Room type	....
Check out	....
Total Nights	....

FLIGHT INFORMATION

Flight N° 1

- Airline Name: ....
- Flight N° : ....
- Departure from: ....
- Arrival to: ....
- Duration: ....
- Confirmation: ....

Flight N° 2

- Airline Name: ....
- Flight N° : ....
- Departure from: ....
- Arrival to: ....
- Duration: ....
- Confirmation: ....

Notes

....
....

DON'T FORGET TO PACK

- **Toiletries**

- **Electronics**

- **Personal Items**

- **Medication**

Made in the USA
Coppell, TX
09 July 2023